W9-BEI-508

I Love You

(LETTERS TO CHILDREN)

From

SWAMI CHINMAYANANDA

CENTRAL CHINMAYA MISSION TRUST

© Central Chinmaya Mission Trust
All rights reserved. No part (either whole or part) may be reproduced, copied, scanned, stored in a retrieval system, recorded or transmitted in any form or by any means including but not limited to electronic and mechanical without the prior written permission of the publisher.

Printed up to	May 2004 Oct.	2010	35,000 copies
Reprint	October	2011	3,000 copies
Reprint	April	2013	3,000 copies

Published by :
CENTRAL CHINMAYA MISSION TRUST
Sandeepany Sadhanalaya, Saki Vihar Road,
Mumbai   400 072, India
Tel. : (91-22) 2857 2367 / 2857 5806
Fax : (91-22) 2857 3065
E-mail : ccmtpublications@chinmayamission.com
Website : www.chinmayamission.com

Distribution Centre in USA :
CHINMAYA MISSION WEST
Publications Division, 560 Bridgetown Pike,
Langhorne, PA 19053, USA.
Phone : (215) 396-0390 / Fax : (215) 396-9710
Email : publications@chinmayamission.org
Website : www.chinmayapublications.org

Printed by :
PRIYA GRAPHICS
Unit No. J - 120, Ansa Industrial Estate,
Saki Vihar Road, Sakinaka, (Andheri)
Mumbai - 400 072. (India)
Tel. No. 6695 9935 / 4005 9936
Email: chinmayapriya@hotmail.com

Price : Rs : 45.00

ISBN: 978-81-7597-223-0

JUST A WORD

When I went into retreat at Uttarkasi, though I was preparing for it for the past one full year, the workload on me was so much and so varied and the relationship between the *Swami* and the Mission members was so intimate and full, that a painful jerk was unavoidable. To cushion off this shock, it struck me that I might write a fortnightly 'letter' to our Balavihar children, who collect themselves in groups all over the country, and where lessons are conducted by the Chinmaya Mission branches. My aim was mainly to educate the *sevaks* and *sevikas* of the Balavihars, and to provide material for the schools, which the Central Chinmaya Mission Trust is patronising, conducting our Balavihar scheme. The teachers can use these letters as the basis for their talks to the children on the

1

moral and religious aspects of human life.

Later on, our Study Group members and Teenagers' Groups started reading these 'letters' in their weekly meetings, and again I had to face and answer volumes of questions raised by them from all parts of the country. I can confess it was no retreat at all in Uttarkasi! Two to three hours I had to be on the grill replying these letters, and the *Brahmacharis* had to type them out through the middle of the night. But the enthusiasm kindled by these letters was a rich reward for all our hours of work on the banks of the Bhageerathi. She glowed upon us – for, isn't she also rushing and humming down the twists and turns of her path to reach, in all love, and serve the people everywhere?

At many centers, the *sevikas* and *sevaks* were devoted enough to conduct writing sessions for the children, where they wrote down what they had understood out of these ideas. A few *sevikas* were kind enough to remember me and knowing that I always love to read the writings of the children, they sent me the best in their Balavihars. In spite of my expressed request, only a few workers found the heart to send the 'attempts' of the children. And that was sufficient. I am convinced that the ideas have gone into them, and I am sure, in time, they will thrive into a lush flowery bower in their growing hearts.

I am thankful to all. Many have worked in this '*Dūta Yajña*', meaning '*yajña* by post' (*dūtaḥ* – mail-carrier). A disciplined, almost 'militant' team of 'activists' in our Mission, all over the country, worked for this 'creative evolution programme'. I sent these letters to the Central Chinmaya Mission Trust office in Bombay. They immediately took copies and posted them to our five zonal secretaries. They prepared the required copies and relayed them to the main branches, and the branches distributed them to the Balavihar Group *sevaks* and *sevikas*. These diligent workers in Balavihars met among themselves, studied these letters, discussed how best they could communicate these ideas to the junior children (6-12) and the senior children (12-16) under their guidance.

3

I must congratulate the entire edifice of our all-India organisation for the clockwork precision with which they worked all along, with so inspiring an enthusiasm. The way Chinmaya Mission fulfilled this programme was in itself an inspiration for me too, here in this valley of quiet inspiration!

Greetings to all from Mother Bhageerathi.

Swami Chinmayananda

Uttarkasi, (U.P.)
9th October 1968.

I LOVE YOU

I

सर्वे भवन्तु सुखिनः
सर्वे सन्तु निरामयाः ।
सर्वे भद्राणि पश्यन्तु
मा कश्चित् दुःखभाग्भवेत् ॥

sarve bhavantu sukhinaḥ
sarve santu nirāmayāḥ,
sarve bhadrāṇi paśyantu
mā kaścit duḥkhabhāgbhavet.

May all become happy. May none fall ill. May
all see auspiciousness everywhere. May none
ever come to any sorrow.

Beloved Children,

Nārāyaṇa! Nārāyaṇa! Nārāyaṇa!
Namaskāram.

I am now here in my simple cottage of meditation on the banks of the Bhageerathi. I am in retreat and *tapas*, to invoke the Lord's Grace on you all. The Lord alone can help you all to grow into big boys and girls; each great and noble, serving the country and its beautiful culture – Hinduism.

The Uttarkasi valley, in the Himalayas, is some 3,800 ft. above sea level, and so, it is cold in summer and very cold, and sometimes snowy in winter. Our divine Mother Ganges constantly rushes down to serve our country and its people everywhere. She is a flow of love itself. When Bhageerathi gushes down, her ice cold waters make an enlivening music. This is echoed by the cloud-capped majestic mountain heights all around. They stand clothed in their pine groves, as if lost in prayers and deep meditation.

Here I was for some years with our Gurudev, Sri Swami Tapovanji Maharaj. He taught me the *Upaniṣads* that tell us of the joyful experiences of our great *Ṛṣis*, who had the direct *darśan* of the Lord of the Universe (*Jagadīśvara*). *Upaniṣads* explain how we too can, through prayer and meditation, realise the Lord of Brindavan in our hearts, if our hearts are sufficiently pure, entirely noble, and supremely courageous.

Our Gururdev taught me also the 'Song of the Lord', the *Bhagavad Gītā*, which describes how we must live in the world, among others, ever serving them in all love.

Gurudev was a very grave and strict teacher, and what he taught once he will no more explain. That was his condition; and I accepted it. And if I happened to forget what had been already taught, I would have to go away; he would no more teach such a forgetful and insincere student. By the blessings of Mother Ganges and my fatherly Gurudev, I remembered everything always. Daily prayers and sincere devotion for the Lord, with an innocent loving heart, make us achieve everything in life.

To a sincere devotee, nothing is impossible. Mere devotion alone is not sufficient. Devotion to the Lord must be ever dancing in our heart, and our hands and legs must sweat in work, our head (intellect) must think well, and thus, 'holding on' to Him in love, let us use all the faculties and powers He has so lovingly given us. Then no one can fail. No one will lose. None can come to sorrow.

Love is the very basis of Hinduism. If you know how to love, you are a great Hindu. All great people have become great because of their love for others. They gained greatness because they learnt to love.

Since love is the heart of Hinduism, we, as children of this mighty culture, must also know what is love, and learn to love all others in this wide world. The Lord is the sheer embodiment of love. If we understand what love is, and teach ourselves to love all, we have served our Lord, Sri Parameshwara. There is no *pūjā* greater than that, no *tapas* more effective. Therefore, children, Love! Love!! Love!!!

It is not possible to discuss love (*prema bhakti*) all of a sudden in a simple letter. But I shall do one thing. Every fortnight I shall write to you. Your group *sevak/sevika* will read out and explain to you my letter every week. All of you must remember all that was taught to you in the previous week. The *sevak/sevika* will ask you questions regarding all the previous letters, as they like. You must be able to answer all those questions. Then they will tell you what I have written to them for the running fortnight. Okay?

From Uttarkasi, some fifty miles north, is the sacred place called Gangotri, the spot where King Bhageeratha did his *tapas*. It is from Gomukh, some ten miles above Gangotri, that Bhageerathi starts her expression as the sacred river. Beyond Gomukh everything is snow, the vast stretches of peaks and peaks over peaks, of endless snow *(hima)* and so the name of this highest mountain of the world is Himalayas – the Abode of Snow.

In Uttarkasi we have the famous temple of Lord Viswanath. Sri Gurudev was a great devotee of this Soumya Kaseesha – Sri Viswanath, and Mother Ganges. It is here, where Parasurama, after his stupendous political and social work, retired to do *tapas* in his mature old age. The neighbouring peaks and small villages tucked away in the valleys have the names of the famous *Rishis* of the *Upaniṣads*. May be, they all had, at one time or other, camped in these places along with their students.

These great masters of perfection taught the students the way of love, and having learnt to live in love, they returned to their places to serve as great Hindus. That is the secret glory of Bharat and its Hindu culture. You must also learn to love, and with pure and chaste love we shall conquer the world and hug man everywhere in love.

Swami Chinmayananda

Uttarkasi (U.P.)
7th May 1968.

II

अलसस्य कुतो विद्या
   अविद्यस्य कुतो धनम्।
अधनस्य कुतो मित्रं
   अमित्रस्य कुतः सुखम्॥

alasasya kuto vidyā
   avidyasya kuto dhanam,
adhanasya kuto mitram
   amitrasya kutaḥ sukham.

Where is education for an idler? Where is wealth for the uneducated? Where are friends for the impoverished? Where is happiness for one who has no friends?

Beloved Children,

Hara! Hara! Hara!
Namaskāram.

In my last letter I told you that love is the very heart of Hinduism. Though we all know what love is, we are shamefully ignorant of the nature of love.

Love, no doubt, is the only solution for man's problem of existence.

At present there are very many unconscious misunderstandings in our vague concept of love. We usually demand that we must be 'loved by others', rather than wanting to 'love others'. We want our elder brothers and sisters to love us, but we don't want to learn to love them.

We generally wait for others to love us, and if we don't get their love, we are unhappy, sad, and feel rejected, unwanted. We never think of going out into the world and giving our love to others. Have you tried this? Have you tried to give love to your friends, relatives and parents? Never! Of that I am sure. Great people alone know how to give love, and in fact, therefore, they are accepted as great.

Others love us. It is not by chance that they come to love us. It is not accidental. If we know how to love, we will be loved by others – this is a law of the Universe.

Don't you ever try to 'fall into' others' love, but as my children, all of you must learn to 'walk out' yourself, to love others. It is active loving, when we give love. Generally we are passive; we cry to 'receive' love.

To love others is an art and we must know its theory and practice, its methods and techniques, in order to master the art of giving love. In music or painting, in engineering or medicine, we must learn the theory, and also for a long time practise them, in order to master any one of them; so too is the great art of giving love to others.

Since we have misunderstood that 'being loved' is love, we always try to be good, cheerful and smart, to dress-up well and to keep beautiful, so that others may love us! In the world, this anxiety to be loved by others makes men run to gain power, wealth, status, position, to undertake daring adventures, and even to perpetrate inhuman cruelties. They believe that these may bring to them love from others.

In love the problem is not 'whom' to love, but it is of 'how' to love. Love is an ability, a capacity in our minds, which is to be systematically cultivated. Once the faculty of love has developed, thereafter, we have the total freedom to love, and any situation is a fertile field for the cultivation of our love.

We really don't know 'how' to love. Our love is disgustingly commercial; we barter away our love for an object or a being, for the benefit or the joy we might get out of the centre of our love. Naturally, in such a relationship, the laws of exchange that govern commodities in a market will come to play – the law of supply and demand!

There is a lot of difference between the epileptic convulsions of love and the gracious surge of love towards things and beings. In short, 'standing in' love is diviner than 'falling in' love. The baser love-emotion is a lightning flash that burns and kills. The nobler love is the warm glow of the springtime sunshine that revives and enlivens.

Two strangers sometimes come together, and often, by accident, they get themselves into an enchanted embrace of beaming love, when all walls of selfishness and vanities fall off, and they both bask in the exquisite sense of fusion of two hearts in love. This is indeed an exciting experience of life. But by its very nature it is not permanent. The charm is lifted. The walls rise up again. They are separated from each other; each will then try to bury his sorrow and disappointment under a mound of calumny against the other. The miracle of fusion is lost. The misery of separateness raises its poisonous hoods!

Around the world, every intelligent man is ever hungry for love; even animals seek and thrive upon love received. Man, irrespective of his race and class, creed and belief, language and nationality, seeks love daily all around him. Yet, only a rare few seem to discover an apparent satisfaction in the personal love relationship. No activity in human life is taken up with so much sincerity and elaborate preparation as man's search for the joy of love, and yet, no enterprise of man fails so consistently, with such regularity, as his quest for love. He merely strives to deserve more and more, he helplessly waits for love to be given to him, to 'receive' love. Alas! None 'gives' love; all are anxiously waiting to 'get' love!

Father demands love. Mother expects love. Brothers and sisters ask for love. You cry for love. All are always disappointed. Nobody seems to get love. There is a universal disappointment. Why?

We must, therefore, enquire into the nature and function of love. We must cultivate a burning aspiration to experience this joy of 'fusion in love' with the world around. Nothing else matters. This alone we need. It is worth any amount of sacrifice.

The end is such a colossal fulfilment that no means is hard enough to be rejected. Such a devoted, intelligent seeker of love can come to know the nature of love and learn the true ways of enduring love.

Children, do you really want to know what love is, and the secret of how to love others? Do you want to discover love for yourself during your long, beautiful and fruitful life?

Swami Chinmayananda

Uttarkasi (U.P.)
22nd May 1968

III

सुखार्थी त्यजते विद्यां
　　विद्यार्थी त्यजते सुखम् ।
सुखार्थिनः कुतो विद्या
　　कुतो विद्यार्थिनः सुखम् ॥

sukhārthī tyajate vidyāṁ
　　vidyārthī tyajate sukham,
sukhārthinaḥ kuto vidyā
　　kuto vidyārthinaḥ sukham.

One who seeks pleasures, renounces studies; one who seeks studies, renounces pleasures. To a seeker of pleasures there is no study; to the studious, where is the time for sense pleasures?

Beloved Children,

Sri Krishna! Sri Krishna! Sri Krishna!
Namaskāram.

I had promised you that we would discuss the nature of love and learn how to love others. Let us first of all carefully observe what is the nature and function of love. Later I shall write to you of the methods of loving the world around you.

Animals have an instinctive sense of possessiveness and a well-developed 'herd love'. When we observe these, we can say that there is love exhibited in their relationship with other animals of their own kind. This sense of blind attachment, and family or caste or national group loyalty is also seen among human beings. But man, in his higher evolution, has gained a greater awareness of himself and of his environments. Man is aware of his own imperfections. He is conscious of the past, excited with the present, and is vaguely worried about his unknown future.

In his grown up, and therefore, more penetrating understanding, he 'knows' that his beloved ones must die one day, and that he himself may have to leave, in his death, all his loved ones. He is alone in the midst of all the multitudes around him. He may have wealth, power, name, fame, achievements, etc., but he is alone, and in that sense of loneliness, he suffers from the panic of separateness.

He is afraid, afraid of himself, afraid of others. The *Upaniṣad Ṛṣis* cry out, "From the other, is all fear."[1] This sense of separateness creates a thousand anxieties, fears, worries and sorrows. In their turn, these drive an individual to be selfish, cruel, angry and sometimes criminal. Love alone becomes, then, the answer for this general problem of human existence.

Without the sense of harmony within, that can be experienced only in the union of love, man suffers from a voiceless pang of

---

1. द्वयात् भयं भवति – *dvayāt bhayaṁ bhavati*

separateness. And this condemns him to an inner sense of loneliness. The *gopīs* felt this anguish when Krishna, the embodiment of love, was not with them. As long as the Flute Bearer was amidst them, so long each of them felt transported into an exquisite state of inner joy and harmony, away from all their sense of loneliness. The despair of Radha, the anguish of devotees, when they find themselves hurled down from their sense of harmony – are all examples of this dark despondency at their own psychological sense of loneliness.

This inner sense of separateness breeds a feeling of shame and a general sense of guilt. Where true love is, none of them can ever come into our heart.[2] Hence Krishna runs away with the clothes of the milkmaids and they had to forget their shame and sense of guilt in their state of 'at-onement' with Him gained through love.

---

2. तत्र को मोहः कः शोकः एकत्वमनुपश्यतः – *tatra ko mohaḥ kaḥ śokaḥ ekatvamanupaśyataḥ*

This is a universal demand: How can one end this sense of separateness and rediscover the fusion in love? How can man learn to rise above his sense of limitations and fears? How can he discover his oneness with the world around him through love? This demand is found in all people, in all periods of history, in all cultures, countries, and races.

As long as we are in our early childhood, there is no sense of separateness. While in the womb, certainly we are one with the mother. And, in the early years of our arrival into this world, we are still entirely one with our mother. But soon, children instinctively start their fight with the mother, rebelling against her sense of total possessiveness. The child's sense of separateness from its parents comes to assert itself – hence its early disobediences. This is natural with all healthy children.

But, with this freedom to revolt, comes the awareness of his separateness as a distinct individual. This sense of separateness brings a painful sense of loneliness and the consequent need for fresh avenues to rediscover his oneness with the world outside, in and through love. The child experiments with new relationships – friends from the neighbourhood, from the classrooms, relatives, teachers and others.

All these attempts to walk out from our own inner life of loneliness into the outer world are undertaken only to discover and gain a union with all, through love. We are essentially one. The experience of the many and so the apparent sense of separateness from all others, are the play of delusion.

The individuality in each of us, in its loneliness, seeks its escape in a thousand ways, and they have all come to be accepted in society. Every new experiment with fresh means for this escape becomes a new fashion. We enthusiastically take up each one of them, and for the time being, feel happy with it, even enthralled by it. But, soon, they get stale, unsatisfactory, and ineffectual. The social search starts again!

Thus the *utsavas* (fairs), congregational singing *(kīrtans)*, elaborate marriage celebrations, festivals such as *Deepavali, Holi* and *Ram-leela,* long and clamorous pilgrimages, sacred baths, *yajñas* and *yāgas,* and nowadays, international sports and games, conferences and exhibitions, military parades and national days (Independence Day, Republic Day), Christmas celebrations, *Jayanti* and *Samādhi* days are all examples, wherein the community tries to escape its sense of loneliness. At these functions and happenings, each man walks out of his self-made inner prison-house of separateness and mixes with all, in the general holiday mood of complete abandon and hilarious joy.

Clubs and dance halls, excessive drinking and drug addictions, anxious hoarding and all over-indulgence of every sort in life, are also 'escapes' for people suffering from this imperceptible sense of agonising loneliness. But, in these, there is generally a lingering sense of guilt, as they are not generally acceptable to the community. Hence, though these are also 'escapes' available for people, yet, even during, and certainly afterwards, there is a backlash of a disturbing guilt-consciousness that silently embitters one's life from one's own within.

In short, all the above general methods of 'escape' pursued by many around the world, in all communities, are, even at their best, extremely unsatisfactory and certainly ineffectual. They are but impotent partial solutions for this grand human problem of existence.

To escape from this shattering experience of loneliness, another method instinctively taken up by a person is to conform to a caste, group, state, or country. He need not then think of himself. He becomes one with all others in his thoughts. He is always in the crowd, one with them all. In his dress, his language, his thoughts, his beliefs, behaviour, actions, work, business, pride, affection – in all his relationships, he is one with the others, and so he persuades himself to believe that he is not separate from others around him in his community.

Driven by the need to escape from the burden that the finite limited consciousness of the ego imposes upon him, as an escape from his sense of loneliness, man associates himself with like-minded individuals. He hopes at least to fortify himself from the sense of dread and dissatisfaction, despair and despondency, depression and dejection. But his hope proves false. He can never find an escape by just functioning with the false 'we' of the group, or by functioning with the false 'I' of the lonely self-centered life.

This is also, then, nothing but an unsatisfactory escape scheme. In spite of them all, something in him compels him to be the distinct individual that he is; each of us is a unique entity. Unless we express this ego personality, we are unhappy.

And thus, though by merging our individuality with all others, we may temporarily escape the pains of loneliness, yet, our ego-personality will assert to express its own unique texture, determined by its distinct demands. Then the sense of separateness shall again precipitate in us, with all its consequent pangs and fears. Therefore, this communal method of 'escape through conformity' is also not sufficient by itself to solve the problem. Had it been totally satisfactory, the rising degree of alcoholism, drug addiction, the alarming number of suicides, in the most developed and highly progressive nations of the world, would not have continued as they do now. Without discovering 'his union with the world around in love', nothing else can save man from his horrid sense of loneliness in himself, even when he is in the midst of a crowded marketplace.

There is this universal demand in the heart of man to seek his identity with all others around him through love. In some it is an urgent, clamorous, conscious demand. In many, it is a slow, silent, unconscious need. But this urge to seek one's fusion with others through love is natural and irresistible in all.

The nature of this love we shall enquire into more closely and discuss in our next letter.

Now all of you write to me in your own words what you have so far understood. Pass it on to the *sevak/sevika* of your Balavihar, who will read them all and send me the best in the group. Will you do all this?

Swami Chinmayananda

Uttarkasi (U.P.)
5th June 1968.

IV

विद्या मित्रं प्रवासेषु
  भार्या मित्रं गृहेषु च ।
व्याधितस्यौषधं मित्रं
  धर्मो मित्रं मृतस्य च ॥

vidyā mitraṁ pravāseṣu
  bhāryā mitraṁ gṛheṣu ca,
vyādhitasyauṣadhaṁ mitraṁ
  dharmo mitraṁ mṛtasya ca.

Your knowledge is your friend in distant lands. Your wife is your friend at home. To the sick, the right medicine is the friend. *Dharma* (righteousness) is a friend even beyond the grave.

Beloved Children,

Hari Śaranam! Hari Śaranam!
Namaskāram.

In my last letter I promised to enquire
more closely into the nature of love. We found
so far that man feels a painful sense of loneliness
in him and to escape from it he tries various
means. All of them are in the end proved
unsatisfactory. They can give him, no doubt,
temporary relief, but, again and again, he starts
feeling that he is alone in himself.

The only moments, when he is happy and
at peace, are the moments when he discovers an
impersonal union with others in love. In the
'fusion of love' with another, man feels uplifted,
enthralled, divinised. This demand is the most
fundamental urge in the human bosom, and this
is the holy passion that holds homes,
communities, nations and races together.

This love is of two distinct types. We may
call them 'the higher love' and 'the lower love'.
The 'higher love' is called *'prema bhakti'*

(devotion) and the 'lower love' is known as 'sneha' (affection). In both prema and sneha, the emotion of love is the same. Only, when the love is directed to a 'higher' object-of-love, it is called prema; and when it is directed towards a 'lower' object-of-love, it is called sneha. Thus, we have 'prema bhakti' towards parents, teachers, country, knowledge, etc., while we have sneha for our friends, brothers, sisters, dogs, cows, flowers, toys, books, etc. Prema is the 'higher love'; sneha is the 'lower love'.

First of all, let us carefully analyse the lower type of love, sneha, and try to understand it thoroughly. Sneha is always for mutual benefit. There is in it a search for a desire-satisfaction. There is togetherness in sneha, but for it to continue, each will always have to enrich the life of the other. The typical example that I can now think of is the mother, and the child in her womb (foetus). The mother's life is, no doubt, enriched by the child within, and the foetus entirely depends upon the mother, for its continued healthy existence. They are separate, but they live life together. In fact, in their togetherness alone is there existence for each. The child cannot live or grow up without the mother, and the mother is not a mother without the child. Each completes the other.

When we come out of the womb also, we enter into such a relationship of mutual dependence with the world around. In our *sneha* with others, each of us tries to complete ourselves. In the *sneha* relationship, we have an abject, hapless, and total dependence upon those whom we love.

Thus, there are many who dread to take any responsibility upon themselves, and so go willingly into the protection of another. Without this protection they feel isolated, lonely, helpless, worried, sad and confused. To such people *sneha* is an escape from their sense of loneliness, their fear of living independently, ever strong and ever free. Here they are demanding love – they need to receive love, they cannot give love.

Such a miserable individual depends entirely upon other objects and beings for his existence. His house, his people, his tea or coffee, his art or work, his money, his friends and relatives, his usual food, clothing, language, temple, river, fields, etc. With these he makes a prison-house for himself and ever willingly suffers in it.

Such a stupid one, as a disciple, comes to depend entirely upon his *Guru* or God, in a disgusting attitude of pathetic slavery. Such a weak one, as a child, clings on to his mother or father to make all decisions for him, to command, to order, to guide, to lead him! They can never grow. They become leeches on others, and they call it 'love'. They are, all through life, mental parasites upon others.

Not only towards parents and *Gurus* is such a relationship maintained, some of us have the same attitude towards God also. "Oh Lord! I am nothing. I am Thy slave. Thou shalt lead me, guide me, help me." This is the shattering expression of *sneha*, and not the calm glow of *prema*, the 'higher love'.

In the Ramanuja philosophy, there is but a slight relief: "Thou art the whole, I am a part of

Thee." Even maintaining the idea that we are parts of Narayana is also *sneha* alone, not real and total *prema*.

In all these instances, the individual is not fully born! In the womb, as the growing foetus, we depended entirely upon the mother, and even when we have come out, many of us are still 'depending' upon things and beings for our existence. This, then, is but a birth from our mother's womb into the world, which to us, is merely yet another bigger and larger womb. To be again born out of this dependence, into the fuller freedom of personality, is called the 'second birth', and true seekers of *Brahman* (Lord), the *brāhmaṇas*, are therefore, called 'twice born'. Those who grow out of the *sneha* relationship into the *prema* identification are true and fit seekers.

This dependence upon others in the world, in order to complete our existence, this *sneha* relationship can be of two kinds – passive and active. In passive *sneha*, the individual clings on, in a slavish attachment to others, and they can thereafter command, order, and lead him, and he will, in implicit abject surrender to another in *sneha*, allow himself to be totally enslaved by this *sneha*, and suffer joyously therein – this dreadful type of mind is noted, and its nature is classified, in modern psychology, as 'masochism'.

The active type of *sneha* is characterised by domination. Such a one, to whom the passive type surrenders, becomes, naturally, aggressive, even cruel in his domineering *sneha*. Such an individual escapes his sense of loneliness by making another as his vehicle to ride on endlessly. The more such devoted persons are around him, the more swelled up he becomes by including them all under his relentless commands, lashing punishments, and awful attitudes. The patriarch in joint families, the overbearing fathers, the terrible mothers, bullying brothers, pompous pontiffs and authoritarian officers are typical examples. All of them are unconsciously trying to seek freedom from their sense of loneliness. The attitude of such minds is called 'sadism' in psychology.

A sadistic person humiliates, hurts, orders and exploits others and feels relieved; stranger still is the fact that the masochistic person, while humiliated, hurt, ordered, and exploited, feels happier, just because he is not alone! Remember, both are suffering from the same sense of loneliness and the consequent fears and despairs, deep beneath their personality layers.

So far I have explained to you the 'lower love' (*sneha*) and it has none of the beauties and glories of the 'higher love' (*prema*). Though you are all children, you must have, in your own minds, seen by now, perhaps your uncle, or father, or mother, or aunt, or brother, or some of your friends, who belong to these two types of 'lower love' (*sneha*). You also must be belonging to either one of the two! Which type are you?

In fact, children, you must understand that both types play in each one of our bosoms. In some, one type is more predominant than the other; that is all the difference. Just as the masochist depends entirely upon the domineering sadist, the sadist himself, in his turn, will be miserable without a masochist to rule over him, to order about or to exploit him constantly. Neither of them is free. Each depends upon the other. This, again, cannot be the final solution for the human problem of loneliness.

In fact, the *Rishis* are never tired of repeatedly asserting that the 'higher love' (*prema bhakti*) alone can help us to escape, fully and entirely, our horrid panic at our own dreadful sense of inner loneliness. Man needs must get out of his own self-made prison-house within, and expand, find his fusion with the entire world around him. This can be achieved only through pure '*prema*-love'.

We shall discuss this 'higher love' in our next letter. In the meantime, try to find out the different types at home and among your friends, and realise to what type you yourself belong.

Swami Chinmayananda

Uttarkasi (U.P.)
20th June 1968.

V

पुस्तकस्था तु या विद्या
    परहस्तगतं धनम् ।
कार्यकाले समुत्पन्ने
    न सा विद्या न तद् धनम् ॥

pustakasthā tu yā vidyā
    parahastagataṁ dhanam,
kāryakāle samutpanne
    na sā vidyā na tad dhanam.

Knowledge that is in notebooks in our shelves, and our money now in the hands of others, both are useless. When the time comes for their use, neither that knowledge nor that wealth will be available.

Beloved Children,

Jaya Jaya Gange Hara Hara!
Namaskāram.

We studied the 'lower love' (*sneha*) in some of its different expressions and found them all unsatisfactory in driving us away from our inner sorrows, on to the amphitheatre of joy and satisfaction. The *Upaniṣads*, the *Gītā*, and the *Purāṇas* not only indicate, in their silent suggestions, but thunder forth the roaring fact that the 'higher love' (*prema bhakti*) can free us from all our sense of separateness and the consequent fears and sorrows of our inner experience of bleak loneliness.

What then is this 'higher love' – *'prema bhakti'*? The emotion is the same in both the higher and the lower kinds of love. But when we direct our love towards a higher, a more inspiring ideal, our minds expand, our faculties broaden, our vision deepens and our efficiency multiplies. Then it is *prema*. When this *prema* is directed towards the Lord, the Divine Essence in man, it is called *bhakti*.

When the same emotion of love goes towards a sense-object or generally towards the external objects of pleasure –things or beings, it slowly shells us into a life of tensions and anxieties, into a prison of sorrows and excitements, pangs and sobs. Then love degrades itself to be of the lower type, *sneha*.

The *prema* type has been glorified in all theistic, religious and great philosophies of the world. Here we give love to Him and expect nothing in return. A true *premi* wants nothing back from Him. The very fulfilment of devotion is in the joy of devotion experienced by the devotee. It asks for nothing. Throats choked with emotion, hearts full of love, tears of joy trickling down their faces, devotees dance in their ecstasy of love for their Lord. And as the whole universe is to them nothing but the Lord's own Form Divine, to the true *'prema bhaktas'*, everything in the Universe is sacred, divine, an object of their deep love and total reverence.

Here the lover is active, and his love is dynamic. He is not waiting to be loved by others. He is not a beggar at the gates of the Temple of Love.

His dynamic love floods forth from his heart towards all, and in its irresistible all-smashing onward dash, it shatters all the walls around others, storms into their hearts, and therein seeks and discovers, a blissful fusion of oneness.

In such dynamic, and, therefore, apparently aggressive love-fusion, the lover ennobles the beloved, and yet, retains his own individuality intact. In such a blessed love-relationship, the two become one, and still, neither dominates the other, nor is anyone rendered a victim of the other.

'Love is active,' according to Hinduism. Be careful – here the meaning of the term 'active' is more significant than what we usually understand.

It is a conscious, wilful 'dashing on' to love, rather than an unconscious accidental 'falling into' love.

It is an aggressively consistent passion 'to give', than a meekly persistent hope 'to receive'.

True loving is not a passive 'taking', but a dynamic 'giving'.

This idea of 'giving' is often dreaded by all. They misunderstand it as a 'giving up' of something, a painful renouncing, a state of being deprived of everything pleasant and sweet. But in our culture it is glorified as *tyāga* −relinquishment. Lord Krishna, in the *Bhagavad Gita*, defines *tyāga* as the 'giving up of all anxiety to enjoy the fruit of actions'. To 'give' love is, therefore, to love everyone without expecting any results, any gains, any profits, but demanding of life your privilege to love all.

Love, when it is true and full, unconditional and joyful, is its own reward − 'love is a fulfilment in itself".* Very few realise

---

* स्वयं फलरूपतेति ब्रह्मकुमाराः − *svayaṁ phalarūpateti brahmakumārāḥ* - from *Narada Bhakti Sutra*.

this; none dare to live it in life. Only those, the special few, who have grown up a little in their inward vision, and so evolved slightly in their spiritual growth, can feel this way, and readily discover the heroism to love, to 'give' love to all creatures. All are but Narayana in manifestation. Then what else can we give to the world, but love?

Some of us love, only if we are also loved in return! That is, we will give love in repayment for the love received! This is a commercial attitude, a mere shopkeeping temperament. Here the demand is subtly for 'receiving' more love than the quantity given. 'I will give only when I receive,' is the expression of our mental weakness.

The sun gives and demands nothing; the earth, the moon, the rains, the spring, the flowers, the rivers, everywhere in nature, among animals and plants, everywhere the universal rhythm is to 'give' lovingly and not to 'demand' love from others.

The former, to give love, is true freedom; the latter, to demand love, is pure slavery.

It is the privilege of man to love. It is the dignity of a devotee to love all as His Creatures. It is the beauty of life that we have this faculty in us to love. We have to cultivate and enrich it in our heart.

A man of commercial temperament, in loving others, expects them to love him back. If he does not receive love, he feels extremely unhappy, terribly disappointed, severely crushed. All of you must have felt this; you must have watched this around you. Hereafter be alert, and be on the lookout for this folly. When you see its play in others, observe how they make themselves unhappy by it. Whenever such a thought rises in you, blast it up immediately.

Repeat at once, in yourself, "I am not a beggar for others' love, I have not come into this world to beg for love, I am here to distribute, to donate, to spread, to shower, to squander love on all others. I am here to flood the world around me with my irresistible love, like Sri Krishna, Sri Ramachandra, the *Rishis*, Sri Buddha, Sri Narayana Guru and others." Nip the wrong thought in its bud. Grow to be my children, each a dynamic lover of the world, marching out to give love and not looking out for receiving love.

Those, who are ready to give love to others only in return for love received, feel cheated if they do not get sufficient return for the love they have already given. This is meaningless. All cannot 'give' love.

Very few are rich in love in themselves. How can they give, who have none in themselves? But you are a Balavihar member, a Chinmaya child. You must develop this capacity to love, and learn to flood life with your love by giving love, asking for nothing in return, expecting nothing, wanting nothing.

Serve all – service of others is the expression of love. Service is the outer expression of the love in your inner heart. See how your mother, father and others serve you, because they love you. We will learn to love all people and animals and plants; for, all are Lord Jagadeeshwara Himself.

Don't feel cheated if others do not give you love. The Lord himself serves us all every moment, even when we don't love him in return! Let us be God-like in our love for others – always and in all ways.

Swami Chinmayananda

Uttarkasi (U.P.)
5th July 1968.

VI

रूपयौवनसंपन्ना
    विशालकुलसंभवाः ।
विद्याहीना न शोभन्ते
    निर्गन्धाः किंशुका इव ॥

rūpayauvanasampannā
    viśālakulasambhavāḥ,
vidyāhīnā na śobhante
    nirgandhāḥ kiṁśukā iva.

They, who have charm and youthfulness, and are born in a great family, yet have no education, do not shine, just like the Kimsuka flowers, which have beauty, but no fragrance.

Beloved Children,

Śrī Rām Jaya Rām Jaya Jaya Rām!
Namaskāram.

We have understood now that to 'give' love is nobler than to 'receive' love. If love comes to us, it is a smile from the Lord, and so it is certainly welcome. We are thankful to the Lord for all the love that we receive. 'But Lord, whether we receive Thy love through people around us or not, to love all other children of Thy creation is our humble *pūjā* at Thy Sacred Feet' – this must be our attitude through our life.

Some people think that to give is an impoverishment, and so they refuse to give even love.

They don't understand that to give love to all others is the only way to enrich life; nothing else can do it as well.

All other glories fade, die away and perish. The divinely sweet beauty of love given, of tenderness shared, of sympathy shown, ever remains untarnished under all circumstances. Adversity cannot dim its brilliance, nor ages destroy its beauty.

Yet, thoughtless people refuse to give love.

To all intelligent people of dynamic character, however, 'giving' has a new meaning and an inspiring suggestion, inherent in that very act.

To 'give' love to others is, to such people, the noblest and the highest expression of their own personality. In the act of giving, they experience a mystic joy of satisfaction, a fulfilment divine.

To 'give' is to them an expression of their creativity and mastery, strength and power, wealth and efficiency. It is to them, the very inspiration in their living, the very breath of their existence.

To 'give' love is to expand. Thereafter the lover functions from two centers, one from within himself and another from the beloved, a centre outside himself.

Thus, in a true giver of love, life quickens, happiness increases, and the sense of loneliness departs, all in a hurry.

When we 'give' love to all, not only does our sense of separateness get lost, but we begin to feel a pride in ourselves for making the world indebted to us, rather than becoming ourselves indebted to the world around. We are the givers of love, the creditors; the creatures around us are the recipients, the debtors.

To receive love from outside us is to be ever indebted to the world around.

This 'giving of love' must be a natural outpouring, as a bird in springtime sings, as the moonlight comforts the earth, as a mother gives her milk to her own child. A natural, effortless, joyous giving must be the gush of love from us unto the world around us.

Whoever gives is rich; the poor cannot give, because he has nothing to give. But one who has got, and yet, is not giving, due to his attachments to his hoards, is also a poor person, indeed. One who has love and yet gives it not, but collects more and more love from others, can never be rich in his life. He is a 'miser' – *kṛpaṇaḥ* – a term used in the *Gita* and in our *Upaniṣads*.

When I say, 'give', I don't mean wealth or your physical strength or power. These, if we have enough to spare, we must give, as an expression of our love. What is to be given is love, a part of ourselves. To give love means to give a part of our own life, share our own joy, cheer, knowledge, courage, etc.

This giving is not to be polluted with even the vaguest traces of any expectations to receive anything in return. Here the giving of love, in itself, is its own reward, its own happiness.

The spontaneity of such happiness enhances the very intensity and depth of satisfaction in it.

Such a dynamic expression of love transforms both the giver and the receiver. Without any reservations, freely, amply, God-like, give. Imitate in this, the extravaganza of a solitary flower sweetening the neighbourhood, even if it is blossoming on a lonely peak!

In such a lavish giving of love alone the fusion of ourselves with the outer world can take place, and in this self-unfoldment, the sense of separateness ends; there is the wondrous joy of a total freedom from loneliness, fear, anxiety and mental depression.

Remember, giving oneself even a little is the expression of true love. The mother's love for the child, a child's love for his parents, a person's love for his country, or community and a devotee's love for the Lord – all are expressed in self-sacrifice, an out-pouring, a liberal giving away.

If one has not cultivated these capacities, one can never be successful in love. We ourselves are always responsible for all our disappointments in our loving. We often hear people complaining, "I did so much for him. I loved him all these years, served him for so many months; I fed him, clothed him, protected him all these days, and yet, he has no love for me now." Indeed it is one of the most painful of worldly experiences, if our friends do not return our love, our brothers do not appreciate our love. But, the cause is indeed in ourselves! We have not given our love in an unreserved way, freely, amply, God-like.

Besides this 'act of giving', there are other dynamic elements in love. However, in all forms of love there are some fundamental factors. And all these basic factors must always be in the bosom of the lover, else the love manifested is false; it then becomes only an apparent illusion of love. Such an impotent love cannot produce any blessings either for the giver or for the receiver of that love.

These basic factors that go into the constitution of love are four in number:

(i)   A sincere anxiety for the beloved
(ii) A sense of deep response
(iii) An ardent attitude of reverence
(iv) A complete understanding of the
      beloved

What these four factors mean, I shall explain in my next letter. Now, merely try to remember them all, these four fundamental factors that form the basis for all deep and growing love.

These are true, whether we love the world around us, or whether our love is turned towards the Lord of the Universe. Love can be enduring and productive only when all these four factors are in the bosom of the 'giver of love'.

Now, children, tell me, have your tried to reach out, of your own accord, to others and love them in all sincerity?

Did you not discover in it a joy?

During the coming weeks, try to love those whom you did not like before. Go and tell that person that you did not like him/her before, and that you have decided to learn to like him/her and give all your love. Try.

You will not only experience a nameless joy in yourself, but you will start feeling proud of yourself, happy with yourself.

Not only do 'you' become happy, but the other person also will slowly change, feel happy first, then ashamed of himself/herself for the lack of love and slowly learn to become a friend again with you.

Carefully, thus, experiment with love. It is a powerful weapon. Nothing can stand against it. It is invincible. The effectiveness of this weapon will depend upon how much love you can give.

Without any reservations, freely, amply, God-like, give.

Swami Chinmayananda

Uttarkasi (U.P.)
20th July 1968

VII

पादपानां भयं वातात्
        पद्मानां शिशिराद् भयम् ।
पर्वतानां भयं वज्रात्
        साधूनां दुर्जनाद् भयम् ॥

pādapānāṁ bhayaṁ vātāt
        padmānāṁ śiśirād bhayam,
parvatānāṁ bhayaṁ vajrāt
        sādhūnāṁ durjanād bhayam.

To the cattle there is fear from storms, to
the lotus there is danger from winter, the
mountains dread the thunderbolt (which in the
past cut off their wings), and good people are
threatened by the evil-minded.

Beloved Children,

Om Namo Nārāyanāya!
Om Namo Nārāyanāya!
Namaskāram.

Have you experimented with love? Did you try to 'give' love? Did you not feel a great wave of joy flooding your heart, when you sincerely poured out your love? This is how love enriches our life.

When we 'give' love, very often, we sincerely believe that we have given love, but we fail to feel the exhilarating joy promised by our *Rishis*. We feel then extremely disappointed. We feel that the philosophers have cheated us.

Sincere love, in a sufficient quantity, when given without reservations, freely, amply, God-like, can never be unrewarding. Joy must follow love given. How then are we to correct the flow of love from ourselves to all others around us?

There are four basic factors in true love. If all of them are there, then your love is full, potent and sincere.

A sincere concern for the happiness of the beloved is the first essential factor of love. A mother loves her children and she is, day and night, anxious for the happiness of her children. If one loves flowers, or a dog, or a cat, or the country, then that love will also be greatly concerned for the welfare and well being of the thing one loves.

Supposing someone says he loves flowers, or a friend, and then forgets to water the flowering plants, or help the friend in trouble, then it is not real love.

One says, 'I love animals,' but whenever he sees a dog, he throws stones at it, beats a cow, catches a butterfly, then his love is not pure.

A boy says, 'I love my father and mother,' and yet, if he disobeys them, brings sorrows to them, is careless of their difficulties, then we say that the boy is cruel, that he has no love.

If you love your sister, you won't pull her hair, or kick her, or snatch anything from her.

When there is love, we become immediately, and automatically, anxious for the happiness of the beloved. In the happiness of the beloved we feel extremely happy, and to a true lover no sacrifice is too much or impossible, if it will protect the beloved.

"The boy stood on the burning deck, when all but he had fled," is a typical example of extreme devotion and love for his father-captain, who ordered him to stand on the deck, at the post of his duty.

Sri Rama loved his mother and father and so he was ready to go into the lonely jungle straight from the luxurious life in the palace chambers in Ayodhya.

A true lover of the country will suffer, will fight, live in poverty, and go without comforts, if that will bring prosperity and glory to his country.

Where there is true love, the lover is never tired of working for and serving the beloved. A loving teacher is never tired of teaching. A loving mother never gets tired of working for her children and their father. A sincere lover of the nation serves day and night the cause of the country.

Love and labour go hand in hand. Where there is love, labour becomes a joy.

One readily labours for that which one loves with all one's heart. And one really loves that for which one labours whole-heartedly.

Therefore, when you love, you must be ever ready to serve the beloved one, and work for the beloved cause. Merely mouthing the words 'I love' is not sufficient. In fact, saying is not even decent, we must express our love in action. That is nobler, diviner, compelling, dynamic.

Let your tongues remain silent; let your hands and legs serve. Let your hearts flood the atmosphere with love. You will then be creating an enchanting magic around you, so

61

that others, however bad they may be, cannot but reciprocate your love.

Secondly, the lover will always have a deep response to the beloved. When one is sincerely anxious for the beloved, there will rise in the lover's mind, an ability to respond readily to the needs and feeling of the beloved. This ability to respond to the needs of others around is the true meaning of 'responsibility' (response-ability).

This term has now come to be understood as an imposition of some heavy duty upon our shoulders by some powers outside ourselves. It is not so. As we grow and expand in love, deep within ourselves, we shall discover that we have become more and more sensitive to uncover the silent needs of others and understand them.

To strive to fulfil for them their needs thus becomes a lover's ecstatic passion.

This is seen most conspicuously in a mother. Her love for her children is immeasurable. Therefore she becomes tuned up to her children. Even when they are away, it has happened millions of times, that the mother feels that the child is not keeping well in the distant land; in psychology this is called 'telepathy'. In varying degrees, when our love is sincere, something in us suddenly tells us that our loved one is happy or unhappy.

That is the ability to respond sympathetically to the beloved. This is a sure sign of true love, and love cannot but generate this secret ability in the heart of the lover.

This is true only when there is deep and sincere love. Else, what we feel is only our own selfish wish. Give love, and be sensitive in your heart, to feel for the unsaid wishes of the beloved. You will find, what I have said above, actually happening many times every day. They surprise not only you, but especially thrill the beloved also. Each time this happens, there will be an explosion of joy in the hearts of both.

Leaders become popular, business men become more successful, officers become lovable, friends become intimate; people become great as social workers, teachers, advocates, engineers, doctors, etc., all because of their unconscious powers to tune in and come to know the needs of others, instinctively. And in all such cases they have naturally, perhaps not by any deliberate training, an intense love for others, or for their work.

All of you, my children, are to become great men and women of India, to raise the country and its culture to its fuller glory, perhaps, as never before. Therefore, you need must cultivate this secret power of love, love that conquers, love that can transform others around you. When we have such an army of real men and women, equipped with sincere love in their hearts, we can march out to give love to the world and lift mankind into a world that is peaceful, prosperous, united, and contented.

I have now explained two of the four basic factors behind love. One cannot be without the other, they are both very intimately connected with each other. We can never have sincere concern for the beloved without 'a sense of deep response' to the beloved. The remaining two factors we will discuss in our next letter.

Each letter coming from here will carry for you more and more understanding of love. You must learn to practise this at home and in school, among your relations and friends. Tell your *sevak/sevika* how far you are successful. Even if you have failed, report to him or her. Your Balavihar *sevak/sevika* will explain to you why you failed.

Swami Chinmayananda

Uttarkasi (U.P.)
5th August 1968.

VIII

नास्ति विद्यासमं चक्षुर्नास्ति
सत्यसमं सुखम् ।
नास्ति रागसमं दुःखं
नास्ति त्यागसमं सुखम् ॥

nāsti vidyāsamaṁ cakṣurnāsti
satyasamaṁ sukham,
nāsti rāgasamaṁ duḥkhaṁ
nāsti tyāgasamaṁ sukham.

There are no eyes that see like knowledge; there are no joys as in truthfulness; there are no pains as in attachment; and there is no bliss as in desirelessness (in true renunciation).

Beloved Children,

Om Namaḥ Śivāya! Om Namaḥ Śivāya!
Namaskāram.

Two of the four fundamental factors that underlie all sincere and deep love were discussed in my last letter. I promised that we would discuss the remaining two factors this time.

We had already found that our 'sincere concern for our beloved' is meaningless if we do not have a 'sense of deep response' to our beloved ones. And this sense of mental attunement, this divine faculty of effortlessly knowing the feelings and needs in the hearts of our beloved ones, can never be generated in full measure unless we have 'an ardent attitude of reverence' towards the loved ones, and this is the third factor in every instance of sincere love given or shown.

We all have 'depths' of personalities in us; yet, we generally meet the world only from our surface. When we are on our surface, we can contact only the surface of the others around us. If we move a little into our own inner nature, we can from there, contact the deeper levels in others. For example, with our eyes we can see others; with our hands we can embrace other bodies; but only from our heart and with our sympathy can we touch the hearts of others and generate their sympathies. With our thoughts we can kindle new thoughts in others and unveil therein, new understanding. Thus, in order to contact the depths in others, we must learn to sing out our love from our own deeper depths.

Reverence is not merely an emotion of love from our heart, or a mere respect born of our intellectual understanding. We can love without respect; we can also respect a person without loving him. I love chocolate but I don't understand what are its ingredients, and how it is made. I understand science and so I respect scientists, but I don't love any scientist.

Where our sense of love, from our mind, and our sense of respect, from our intellect, meet to merge together, at one and the same altar, the feeling so generated, at the confluence of love and respect, is called 'reverence'. This can be generated and maintained only by an integrated mind-intellect equipment in our selves.

Thus, when we have a deep sense of reverence for life and all living creatures, then alone our love for others becomes potent. I may love you, but in case I have no respect for you, certainly you will always feel insulted at all my sincere and loving approaches. The lover must have a subtle sense of reverence towards the beloved. If you love your mother or father or brother, but you have no reverence for them, they will not at all be influenced by your love. Loving the world without reverence for life and people is like a delicious curry, well cooked and cleanly served, but without salt!

In the factors of reverence, the love-aspect is generally known to us. The moment we hear the word 'respect' we misunderstand it to mean a feeling mingled with fear, awe and distance between ourselves, and the object of our reverence. This is wrong; the root from which the word 'respect' comes is *'respicere'* meaning 'to look at'.

To respect a person, therefore, means to 're-cognise' him as he actually is. To show respect means to help him grow and unfold himself, in himself, by himself. The parents should 'respect' their children; teachers must have 'respect' for their students.

We are not able to give others this true respect, because we do not feel one with them. What we generally call love is only an attempt to make use of the loved one for our purpose! Thus, we strive to make of him/her what 'we' want him/her to be! This is not love; a true lover sees the beloved with perfect objectivity, and without interfering with the personality of the beloved one, the lover, with his ungrudging love, blesses the other to grow, unfold and fulfil by himself/herself.

Love, when it is pure, has a revitalising effect upon others, and in the presence of such a truly loving one, others grow and expand into a healthier state of being. Without deep reverence to the beloved, such a refreshing stream of love cannot flow from the heart of the lover.

Generally, we need help from others, to live effectively and continue functioning efficiently as a psychological entity. We are very rarely, if ever, free in our mental life. We need others and their applause, their acceptance and kindness, their sympathy and love etc. to scaffold our individuality, our ego. In short, we want to be loved by others.

To give love, we must become independent in ourselves and be a pillar in life, allowing others to hold on to us. Only such an individual, who needs no crutches for his own existence, can have the power to 'give' love. All others are only 'receivers' of love.

When a person, who has such an inner strength of personality and a healthy sense of deep reverence to life and people, gives love, it transforms the world of creatures in his orbit.

He constantly throws around him a vibrant light of wondrous enchantment, himself forming an island of peace and contentment in the stormy life of tumultuous fears and smashing confusions all around him.

To summarise, dear children, we have so far discussed that to be a dynamic person of strength and leadership, living a rich life of service, ever looking out for chances to give love to all others, we must have (i) a sincere concern for the beloved, (ii) a sense of deep response, and (iii) an ardent attitude of reverence to life and the world around us.

Without reverence, the response will not be satisfactory, and where there is no ability to respond, there can be no deep concern for the beloved. Now, the ardent attitude of reverence can spring up only where there is full understanding, and so, the fourth basic factor in love is (iv) 'a complete understanding of the loved one.'

Concern for, response and reverence to, the beloved – all can be only false and empty, blind and foolish, if they do not flow from a firm and sure understanding of the beloved thing or being.

In *Narada Bhakti Sutra*, the means of developing love-divine have been described, and the very first *Sutra* in this discussion says, "Some say understanding alone is the means."* True. Without a general knowledge of the object of our love, we cannot feel love, and with a deeper understanding, our love also deepens and widens.

A superficial knowledge is not sufficient; an understanding in us, that pierces through the outer layers and penetrates into the core of the beloved's personality alone, can assure from us a steady reverence, a ready response and a tidy concern for the 'object' of our love.

In order to enter into another's being, one must lose one's own selfishness, and learn to merge, to be one with the beloved, be it a

---

* तस्याः ज्ञानमेव साधनमित्येके – *tasyāḥ jñānameva sādhanamityeke - Sutra* 28.

community, a nation, or the world. So long as we remain overly concerned with our own comforts and physical happiness, we can never give effectively our love to others, expanding into the greater and the nobler spiritual dimensions in ourselves. In this inner expansion alone can the blistering sense of separateness end and its suffocating sorrows, fears and anxieties finally depart from our bosom.

This understanding can come to us only through the words of the *Rishis* and by consistently applying our present abilities to love others. The analytical methods of modern physiology and psychology are not efficient enough to reach the depths. This is the instinctive method of a crude childhood – a child will crush a flower, will smash a toy, will tear a thing, in its natural attempt to understand the objects in front of it. It will pluck the hairs; pull the ears of a cat or a dog. It will bite, lick, throw, beat, scratch, kick etc. in order to gain a knowledge of the world around it. These crude methods on a larger scale constitute our scientific paths of analysis, including vivisection. This is incompetent in unravelling the mystery of man's personality. To plumb the depths, love alone is the means.

At the levels of the body or mind or intellect, we understand each other, and our understanding provides us only with the information regarding the physical, mental and intellectual contents in others. Even here they are vague, uncertain, and largely erroneous. From the Self alone all is known in all its entirety, and only thereafter, and with reference to it, can we correctly perceive the relative positions of all other factors of personality in man.

This hunger to know our selves and others was ever with man, and the Delphic motto declared it: 'Know Thyself'.

Until we discover this Spiritual Centre in ourselves, the God in us, we will be confused, miserable, unsatisfied and disturbed, an enigma to ourselves and to others.

Love alone is the path; it alone has the necessary power to reach the required depth to rediscover the Real Essence in us, and others around us, the One Infinite Self.

See, children, how intimately connected are religion and our happiness in life, our communal and national living – why, even world peace and prosperity. Without mutual love, we can make a hell of this world; with true love world can be a heaven. In order to give love, we must have a rich treasure of all these four fundamental factors of love in us.

Ultimately, love helps my understanding of myself, and the world around me – the Self in me is the Self everywhere.

Swami Chinmayananda

Uttarkasi (U.P.)
20th August 1968.

IX

यौवनं धनसम्पत्तिः
      प्रभुत्वमविवेकिता ।
एकैकमप्यनर्थाय
      किमु यत्र चतुष्टयम् ॥

yauvanaṁ dhanasampattiḥ
      prabhutvamavivekitā,
ekaikamapyanarthāya
      kimu yatra catuṣṭayam.

Youthfulness, wealth and property, power, indiscretion – each one can destroy a man. What should we say of him who has all the four?

Beloved Children,

Jaya Jaya Jagadīśa Hare!
Namaskāram.

No art can grow and shine forth without (1) self-discipline, (2) concentration, and (3) total dedication. Endless practice is needed to perfect oneself in any art – music, painting, medicine, sculpture or dance.

To live rightly is itself an art – to give love to others, and thus to enrich life around you, by your own right living, is the subtlest of all known arts in the world.

You, my children, are now being taught this greatest of all arts, the 'Art of Giving Love'. Buddha, Christ, Mahatma Gandhi, Albert Schweitzer, the *Rishis* of the *Upanishads*, the three great *Acharyas*, Swami Vivekananda, Sri Ramakrishna Paramahamsa, Sri Narayana Guru of Kerala – were all mighty artists in giving love and transforming life upon this earth with their love.

Love we all have. In fact all our activities spring forth from love; however cruel or criminal the act may be, when we enquire into its motive, deep beneath it all, is the love of the individual for himself, or for his dear ones.

'The art of loving' essentially consists in knowing how to cultivate the love-sentiment in us and how to give it readily and freely to others around us always.

To love another, we must curb our selfishness, vanity, greed and passions. So long as we have these, we have love only for ourselves. And often, what we have, may not be found sufficient even for ourselves, and we will have to demand that others lend us liberally their love also, so that we may fulfil our requirements from others around us!

To curb these negative temperaments is to cultivate virtues like large-heartedness, humbleness, kindness, and a calm composure of the heart within – continuously. This is self-discipline.

Again, practice of spreading love is to be consistently pursued even under very trying circumstances. Often, in our honest attempt to give love to another, the individual himself may misunderstand our attitude, and we may receive but curses from him for all our affection shown, tenderness expressed or even love given. Silently we must pocket the insults and learn to love more and more. This is self-discipline.

Sometimes we are not in a mood to love; we may be ourselves shattered within, tired mentally or fatigued physically. But a true lover has no excuse for not being able to give love to all. To maintain our love continuously towards our chosen ideal is 'self-discipline'. During each occasion of loving others, we must be sensitive enough to feel its weaknesses and strengths, its imperfections and perfections. To notice them in our own self-analysis is to polish our ways for future occasions. To learn from our own experience is the best school for all arts. This is self-discipline.

No artist can grow and reach out to any amount of mastery in his art if he has not sufficient amount of 'concentration'. Concentration is the capacity to continue applying our mind at a point of attention in spite of all possible distractions and disturbances, obstacles and impediments. This is natural in all great artists, and all apprentices will have to cultivate it. When the aspirant has discovered in himself a great enchantment for the art, he gains the necessary concentration in himself, for that art. This is to be zealously cultivated, constantly practised and carefully preserved.

While growing in the path of 'giving' love to others, we must have both strict self-discipline and high 'concentration'.

Lastly, we must approach this art with all seriousness, not as a hobby, but as our life's sole mission, and, therefore, there must be in us a sense of 'total dedication' to it. The intensity of our spirit of dedication, and consequently, our ability to make any amount of cheerful sacrifices, in pursuing this grand 'art of giving love', will determine the degree of our success in it.

One who knows how to give love is a living God upon earth. To gain this mastery is the highest achievement in life.

Thereafter, you are never lonely – the whole world is yours.

The world itself can never stand apart from such a person.

Naturally, in gaining such a divine state of kingship in life, for winning such a supreme status of sovereignty over the world of existence, we will not be the losers, even if we are to make the maximum sacrifices.

(1) Self-discipline, (2) high concentration and (3) a sense of total dedication are all auxiliary factors. They prepare us to give love. But nothing helps us in the art of loving as practice itself. Love breeds upon love itself.

Narada Bhakti Sutra clearly declares that to love is the only means for cultivating love.*

Our first few attempts may not be quite successful. But let us teach ourselves by repeated falls; watch how a child learns to walk – what industry, consistency, courage and heroism! How many falls, yet up again stands the baby, to try once again to walk by himself. And the child, in the end, masters it all by himself; so too, in 'the art of giving love' to others in the world, he who has the heroism, masters it through some of his early falls and stumbling.

Again, Narada insists that love increases with an understanding of the virtues of the other (or Lord) and by glorifying them.* Here the word meaning but begs the solution; we must strive to reach at the subtle significance. There is none without some noble traits. Let

---

* स्वयं फलरूपतेति ब्रह्मकुमाराः - *svayaṁ phalarūpateti brahmakumārāḥ*

* भगवद्गुणश्रवणकीर्तनात् - *bhagavad-guṇa-śravaṇa-kīrtanāt*

us discover them, and thereafter, let us glorify them. The best glorification of a virtue in another is not by words or speech. It must be in imitating them and applauding liberally those persons for their simple noble qualities. Love will flood out from us for them, for those very virtues, which we first detected in them, helped us to cultivate them within ourselves!

All these need self-discipline. If we are full of vanity, we will not have the large-heartedness to overlook the weaknesses and faults in others and detect the traces of goodness in them.

We needs must have great patience. For, the world will not understand our sincerity. They will doubt our motives. The more the evil in a man, the less he will respond to sincere and pure love. Such an instance of larger resistance to love should be, to a dynamic lover, an appetising challenge, to be faced and heroically won over.

My dear boys and girls, remember this. To love others has been the function of the greatest devotees. To give love to others is the privilege of the few. The large majority of creatures are beggars for love. They demand love. They expect to receive love.

But you are my children and, therefore, I want you all to be true *Bharatiyas*. Here, in this country, our culture insists on a life of giving, and conquering the chastened world of beings with our developed and enhanced love-potential.

If we have the *Īśvara-bhāva*, the divine attitude that the universe around us, extending all around to infinite distances, is but Sri Narayana's own form, the love we give to His creatures becomes our love-offering unto Him.

Swami Chinmayananda

Uttarkasi (U.P.)
5th September 1968

X

हस्तस्य भूषणं दानं
     सत्यं कण्ठस्य भूषणम् ।
श्रोत्रस्य भूषणं शास्त्रं
     भूषणैः किं प्रयोजनम् ॥

hastasya bhūṣaṇaṁ dānaṁ
     satyaṁ kaṇṭhasya bhūṣaṇam,
śrotrasya bhūṣaṇaṁ śāstraṁ
     bhūṣaṇaiḥ kiṁ prayojanam.

Charity is the ornament for the hand;
truthfulness is the necklace that decorates the
neck. *Śāstra* (Scripture) is the adornment for
the ears – then of what use is jewellery?

Beloved Children,

Hari Om. Hari Om. Hari Om.
Namaskāram.

The Lord created this world so that His
creatures may live in the cohesiveness of the
embrace of love. The Lord in our heart is the
very centre of all love (*sarva-premāspadatvāt*) and
hence we express, in all our love outside, only
our love for our own Self. The outer world is
but an expression of the One Self, which is in
all – Sri Narayana.

So long as this deep understanding of
God as our own Self in us, has not risen in us,
our love for the world around us cannot be free
and universal. It will not have the width, the
height, and the depth to accommodate all.
When the love in us is not cultivated to its most
extravagant dimensions, how can we afford to
'give' love to others? We too shall only be needy
beggars crying for love, among the endless
multitudes of beggars, crowding all over the
surface of this globe. Without love for God, love
for man becomes sentimental and it can never

be a true giving of love; apparently we may be 'giving', but deep down there will be a demand for 'receiving' love.

This love for the Lord is of different textures, depending upon the growth and development of the individuals and the society in which they happened to grow up. In the earliest stages man feels ardently his oneness with the nature around him, even though he has grown out of it as an independent type, evolved out of the levels of the trees and the animals. Yet, in his early stages, man tries to maintain his sense of identity with them; hence his worship of trees and animals. Even now, among the tribal religions, we find this very prominently cultivated.

As man grows under the pressures of his needs and the visions of his intellect, he discovers more and more abilities in himself to create things by himself. At this stage he becomes more and more conscious of himself and his separateness from other things and creatures in the world. It is at this stage that man comes to make His God in stone, wood or metal. The idol worship starts then.

Even here, at the earliest stages of his history, man seems to have worshipped his God as Mother. Children always love the mother first. In this 'Divine Mother' concept, She loves Her children, just because they are Her children, and not for any other reason. The Divine Mother is ever all-loving, and whatever we may do, we have only to cry out "Maa-Maa...' or 'Mummy...' but once, and She will forgive everything and gather us into Her protective, nourishing bosom.

From these mother-centered days religion slowly moved to the father-centered attitude, wherein God comes to be considered as a strict, but kindly, father. He expects us to obey His laws, to live as His 'image', to fulfil what He expects of us. If we default in any of His expectations, no doubt, He punishes severely; but if obedient and industrious, humble and productive, then He makes us His successors!

In main, almost all the great religions are now at this stage. Yet, it must be admitted that the Mother concept of God will never leave the world, as long as man craves for the mother's unquestioning, all-giving, doting love.

Thus, we may say that there was a movement from the matriarchal to the patriarchal religions. Even in the patriarchal religion, as man grew up into a fuller awareness of his own independent and separate existence, and as he explored slowly more and more of his own abilities and capacity, in the consciousness of his fuller stature, his concept of God also changed.

From an unrelenting disciplinarian, an almighty tyrant, a merciless power that rules man with dictatorial whims, punishing ruthlessly, demanding unquestioning submission to His rule and obedience to His laws, the God-concept evolved into a Divine Power, of all-mercy, all-love, all-justice.

This shows the growth of the child into its adolescence, and from his adolescent stage of fear of the father, he grows to reach the responsible state of youth, when he becomes mature enough to recognise the reasonableness of his father's authority, the blessings of His rules, and the justice of His laws. He is now able to recognise the anxious, loving, dedicated benefactor in his apparently rude and fierce father.

The final stage is when the youthful man grows into full maturity, when the father becomes old, and the son comes to feel his intimate identity with his father. Religion, at its highest, recognises this noblest relationship between the devotee and the Lord – a relationship of agreement, a sense of supreme nearness. Ultimately, he discovers his total identity with Sri Narayana, the One Infinite Reality, the Self in All.

This is not a mere hypothesis, an idle supposition, or an empty theory. According to the type of people that constitute a given community, in any given era of history, these different types of 'relationships' between man and God are found emphasised. Thus Madhvacharya emphasised that the devotee and the Lord are ever separate – the *Dvaita* philosophy.

Ramanujacharya, at yet another period of recent Hinduism, declared that man is not 'totally different' from the Lord, but that he and his Lord have a 'part-and-whole' relationship. The Lord is the 'whole', while the devotee is a 'part' of Him – the *Viśiṣṭādvaita*.

Adi Sankaracharya insisted that ultimately the devotee, in his essence, is identical with the Supreme – the *Advaita* philosophy.

We can surely say that these three *Acharyas* are not contradicting among themselves. We first cling on to the father, fearing him, and then, as we grow, we learn to feel that we, as his children, have some rights of our own in our homes. Only when we have grown up fully do we realise that father and children are not separate, but that our interests are ever identical.

The story of the development of religion and man's concept of God is the natural story of our own slow and steady growth in life. This you all must carefully learn. You must, many times, independently think over these ideas yourself. As your understanding of your parents becomes more and more complete, your relationship with them also changes. So too, when our knowledge of the Infinite Truth deepens, our relationship with God also gets transformed, until we discover our total identity with Him, who is the Essence in all things and beings. This is the culmination of love, the fulfilment of love.

Your *sevak/sevika* will explain all this to you. You must clear your own doubts by fearlessly asking him/her questions. He/she will explain everything to you. See in your mind the entire logic of this gigantic picture of the history of the growth of religions.

Swami Chinmayananda

Uttarkasi (U.P.)
20th Sept. 1968

XI

नरस्याभरणं रूपं
      रूपस्याभरणं गुणः ।
गुणस्याभरणं ज्ञानं
      ज्ञानस्याभरणं क्षमा ॥

narasyābharaṇaṁ rūpaṁ
      rūpasyābharaṇaṁ guṇaḥ,
guṇasyābharaṇaṁ jñānam
      jñānasyābharaṇaṁ kṣamā.

Stature is the charm of a man. Character is the charm in the stature. Knowledge is the charm in character. And forgiveness is the glory of knowledge.

Beloved Children,

Cidānanda rūpaḥ Śivoham Śivoham
Namaskāram.

We had discussed in an earlier letter that there is a gulf of difference between the 'lower love' (*sneha*) and the 'higher love' (*prema*). The highest love is when we seek, discover, and experience our essential oneness with the very substance of Truth, the Lord. It is called devotion (*prema bhakti*).

The various shades of love are unconsciously and irresistibly practised by all, in order to escape the stifling sense of separateness in us, and its consequent fears and despairs. These drive each one of us into neurotic conditions of unutterable sorrows. There is no exception here. This is universally applicable to all. But so long as our love is 'objective', it is, even at its best, very unsatisfactory. Then our love depends upon the nature and quality, texture and behaviour, fulfilment and use of the 'object of love'. It is but a conditional love, conditioned by our attitude, and the nature of the 'object' that we love.

This is a 'slave love', not a free love. If the situation or the mood changes, either in the bosom of the lover, or in the beloved, the wondrous thrill of love between them gets lost. In fact, in such a case, the love is not pure; for, where love has a desire to be fulfilled, a gain to be had, a purpose to be served, then it is 'lust'. The algebra of love says:

Pure Love (*prema*) + desire (*rāga*) = lust (*kāma*). Therefore, it becomes evidently clear what 'pure love' is.

Pure Love (*prema*) = lust (*kāma*) − desire (*rāga*). Hence Krishna describes Himself as *kāma, rāga vivarjitam* − I am lust without desire.

This desire prompted love is an octopus love. The beloved is sucked dry and destroyed by the 'lust' in the lover. And the lover, for all his love, gets only the hatred of the beloved as his reward, and the subjective punishment of added restlessness in himself. Never can he find satisfaction in such a love. He seeks love, but he will never discover it. He, in his 'lust', searches for the many in the One.

In true love (*prema*), there are no desires to be satisfied, no demands to be met, no vulgar expectations to be fulfilled. It is pure *prema*, which is its own fulfilment, its own reward. To love thus, with all our heart, is the privilege of our grown up human stature, our achieved evolutionary growth. Narada describes such an all-inspiring, self-expanding love as '*anu-raga*'. This is the search for the One in the many. And the Devarshi, without mincing matters, openly confesses that such pure love is seen manifest only in some rare bosoms.*

Each lover has his own specific way of expressing his love. It all depends upon the

---

* दृश्यते क्वापि पात्रे - *dṛśyate kvāpi pātre – Narada Bhakti Sutra*

psychological type to which the individual belongs. There are some among us, who love in their world the father more than anyone else. Others love the mother more. Some love their friends. Yet others love their master or boss. These are the various 'attitudes' in love. Paternal, maternal, brother, slave, master, friend – these represent some of the more prominent attitudes of love commonly met with in society. The 'secret love' attitude and the wifely attitude are also not uncommon.

All these attitudes can be encouraged. Each one of them can develop this love potential in us, by loving others in our own particular characteristic attitude of love. Once the restraining dam that holds our love in our bosom is burst, we shall be surprised at our own infinite capacity to love. We shall then find our fuller existence in life, through that all-consuming total love for all.

In this grand scheme of self-expansion, gained through the discovery of our own identity with others, there is no outer limit.

There is no power to restrain it, except our own desires or passions. Therefore, until we purify our own hearts, we will not be efficient instruments to 'give' love.

Devotion to Sri Narayana is also a means to cultivate love within. To 'hear' His glories, to 'sing' about His beauties, to 'reflect' upon His love, to 'meditate' upon His Presence within us, are some of the ways by which a devotee grows in his love for Him.

The Lord is not only a 'heaven- residing', 'other - worldly' Lord, but He is right here, everywhere. When, out of gold some ornaments are made, all such ornaments are nothing but gold. When the universe has emerged from the Lord, who 'was' before all creation, everything in the universe can only be His Essence alone. To recognise Him in and through the world, and to adore Him with our sincere and active love for all living creatures, is the highest *pūjā*, the noblest prayer.

Please, children, don't misunderstand from what I just now said, that the world 'is God'. The world 'is not' God, the world 'has' God.

Seek Him through love. Search for Him through your devotion. Invoke Him with prayer. And finally meet Him in your meditation.

No single individual is God, but all are His expressions. Your mother's hair is not your mother, but it is her own extension. Your leg is not you, but you are in your leg. Milk 'is not' butter, but milk 'has' butter. Now do you understand?

As butter is in milk, so is Lord Parameshwara in the world. As we churn and take the butter from the milk, so too, by our love we must get at the Lord, now playing hide and seek with us all around us. Catch Him with your goodness, cheer, joy and love for all.

To watch for Him in the day-to-day play of all the happenings around us is a thrilling game, an endless joy and a life-long entertainment.

Thereafter, joy is no joy – sorrow is no sorrow!

In playing a game, the excitement of the game is its own reward. We may fall. We don't worry. We may be knocked down and even get hurt. We don't care. We may win. It is of no consequence. We may lose. It doesn't matter. If we had a good, hard and bright game, that in itself is the real thrill of the game.

To one who knows how to 'give' love in life, to him all his life becomes an exciting game.

Swami Chinmayapanda

Uttarkasi (U.P.)
5th October 1968.

XII

स्वगृहे पूज्यते मूर्खः
स्वग्रामे पूज्यते प्रभुः ।
स्वदेशे पूज्यते राजा
विद्वान्सर्वत्र पूज्यते ॥

svagṛhe pūjyate mūrkhaḥ
svagrāme pūjyate prabhuḥ,
svadeśe pūjyate rājā
vidvānsarvatra pūjyate.

The fool is worshipped only in his house. The rich man is respected in his own village. The king is honoured only in his own kingdom. But the wise man is worshipped, respected and honoured in all places, at all times, under all conditions.

Beloved Ones,

Om Namo Bhagavate Vāsudevāya!
Namaskāram.

The measure of our freedom is the measure of our ability to 'give' love. It is our inner shackles that take away from us all our love and make us hungry and thirsty for love from others. Therein, man becomes a slave to the world of tempting objects and charming beings.

Such a person, thereafter, becomes a passive or an active 'receiver' of love, a 'masochist', or a 'sadist'. Both live indeed a miserable existence. Such persons can never grow to be great men and women of their era.

You, my children, are being trained to be world-renowned artists, writers, scientists, leaders, and spiritual masters. Such a spectacular self-expansion cannot be had if we grow to be beggars of love from money, power, or other lifeless things and from a host of living beings.

Without a full spirit of sacrifice don't try to walk love's footsteps. We must be able to renounce everything; if need be, our very life for 'giving' love to others.

Buddha showed it, Christ followed it. All the mighty saints lived this spirit every moment of their lives.

Without such a firm determination to love, how can we have the world-transforming heroism, the life-giving courage, to live above all temptations, above all chains of attachment, and embrace the entire universe?

True, in spite of all our best efforts, we may slip now and then. But that need not worry us. We are imperfect ones trying our best to gain perfection. Let every slip in us be an education for us. Let us grow and expand, ultimately to improve, to shine out.

The day you take up this policy of 'giving' love, rather than 'demanding' it, that day you would have rewritten your entire future destiny.